GUIDELINES FOR THE ASSESSMENT OF GENERAL DAMAGES IN PERSONAL INJURY CASES

GUIDELINES FOR THE ASSESSMENT OF GENERAL DAMAGES IN PERSONAL INJURY CASES

Twelfth Edition

Compiled for the

Judicial College

by

THE HON. MR JUSTICE BURNETT;

PETER CARSON, SOLICITOR;

STUART MCKECHNIE, BARRISTER;

STEVEN SNOWDEN, BARRISTER;

RICHARD WILKINSON, BARRISTER

Foreword by The Hon. Mr Justice Ramsey

OXFORD
UNIVERSITY PRESS

OXFORD
UNIVERSITY PRESS

Great Clarendon Street, Oxford, OX2 6DP,
United Kingdom

Oxford University Press is a department of the University of Oxford.
It furthers the University's objective of excellence in research, scholarship,
and education by publishing worldwide. Oxford is a registered trade mark of
Oxford University Press in the UK and in certain other countries

© Judicial College, 2013

The moral rights of the authors have been asserted

Twelfth Edition published in 2013
Impression: 1

Crown copyright material is reproduced under Class Licence
Number C01P0000148 with the permission of OPSI
and the Queen's Printer for Scotland

Published in the United States of America by Oxford University Press
198 Madison Avenue, New York, NY 10016, United States of America

British Library Cataloguing in Publication Data
Data available

Library of Congress Control Number: 2013943729

ISBN 978–0–19–968782–4

Printed in Italy by
L.E.G.O. S.p.A. – Lavis TN

Contents

Foreword to the Twelfth Edition of the Judicial College's Guidelines for the Assessment of General Damages in Personal Injury Cases

These Guidelines, now in their twelfth edition, are well established as the source of essential information for judges and practitioners when considering awards of damages in personal injury cases. The guidance becomes ever more necessary as awards of damages become more complex and the challenges of litigation increase.

Over the past year the implementation of the Jackson reforms has had a number of major impacts on those who practise in the personal injuries field. The removal of the recoverability of success fees on conditional fee agreements and of after-the-event insurance premiums, together with the ban on referral fees has had a major impact on the way in which personal injury litigation will be funded. In the short term there will be a large number of cases dealt with under the regime as it existed before 1 April 2013, judging from the number of CFAs and ATE policies entered into just before that date. In the longer term, new ways have to be found to fund litigation. Some changes have been made to mitigate the position. It has to be seen how the third party litigation funding industry develops and how far that sector provides new funding opportunities whilst only the subject of voluntary regulation.

The need for claimants to have ATE insurance is now greatly lessened, if not wholly avoided, by qualified one-way costs shifting (QOCS). It is also acknowledged that under the new regime with the use of CFAs or damages-based agreements or even traditional arrangements, successful parties will have to pay some costs out of the damages recovered. This led to the implementation of the Jackson recommendation that general damages should rise by 10% in *Simmons v Castle*. Obviously, as stated elsewhere in these Guidelines, this has added a degree of complication to this publication.

The Jackson reforms do not just change the funding regime, they also aim to reduce the overall costs of litigation by changes to case and costs management. Much time and cost is wasted by the failure of parties to comply with orders, rules and practice directions. The courts are therefore tightening up on such compliance and will be far less willing to grant further time or relief from sanctions. To control costs there are changes to disclosure, witness statements and expert reports. There has to be information, at an early stage, about the scope and cost of disclosure so that the court can determine the appropriate disclosure order, if any. Witness statements have to be focused on necessary factual issues. The court will need to know the scope and cost of expert evidence before it gives permission.

Parties are being encouraged to use ADR. New provisions add an extra 10% to claimant's damages if the defendant fails to beat a claimant's Part 36 offer. Taken with recovery of costs, up to a limit, for successful defendants in the QOCS rules, this changes the dynamics of Part 36 offers in personal injury claims.

Probably the most important new area is the requirement to manage costs so that they are proportionate. This involves parties producing costs budgets at the beginning of proceedings so that the litigation is concluded at a level of recoverable costs in accordance with that budget. The budget is set at levels of cost which have to be proportionate to the claim, taking into account the value of the claim, complexity and other defined matters. This is aimed at avoiding cases where the costs at the end are, for example, many times the sum in issue, so that the costs rather than the damages become the real issue.

With the reforms only a few months old and with many cases still continuing under the old funding arrangements it will be some time before the full impact of the reforms can be assessed. They form part of the process started by the Woolf reforms and if successful will go a long way to achieving the aim of access to justice at proportionate cost—the brief given to Lord Justice Jackson. There are evident challenges and uncertainties for those who practise in the personal injury field but those will be justified if that aim is achieved.

Vivian Ramsey

Foreword to the First Edition by Lord Donaldson of Lymington

Paradoxical as it may seem, one of the commonest tasks of a judge sitting in a civil court is also one of the most difficult. This is the assessment of general damages for pain, suffering or loss of the amenities of life. Since no monetary award can compensate in any real sense, these damages cannot be assessed by a process of calculation. Yet whilst no two cases are ever precisely the same, justice requires that there be consistency between awards.

The solution to this dilemma has lain in using the amount of damages awarded in reported cases as guidelines or markers and seeking to slot the particular case into the framework thus provided. This is easier stated than done, because reports of the framework cases are scattered over a variety of publications and not all the awards appear, from the sometimes brief reports, to be consistent with one another. Furthermore some of the older cases are positively misleading unless account is taken of changes in the value of money and the process of revaluation is far from being an exact science.

It was against this background that the Judicial Studies Board set up a working party under the chairmanship of Judge Roger Cox to prepare 'Guidelines for the Assessment of General Damages in Personal Injury Cases'. It was not intended to represent, and does not represent, a new or different approach to the problem. Nor is it intended to be a 'ready reckoner' or in any way to fetter the individual judgment which must be brought to bear upon the unique features of each particular case. What it is intended to do, and what it does quite admirably, is to distil the conventional wisdom contained in the reported cases, to supplement it from the collective experience of the working party and to present the result in a convenient, logical and coherent form.

There can be no doubt about the practical value of this report and it has been agreed by the four Heads of Division that it shall be circulated to all judges, recorders and district judges who may be concerned with the assessment of general damages in personal injury cases. We also consider that it should be made available to the two branches of the practising profession and to any others who would be assisted by it.

Judges and practitioners will, as always, remain free to take full account of the amount of damages awarded in earlier cases, but it is hoped that with the publication of this report this will less often be necessary. They will also need to take account of cases reported after the effective date of the working party's report since that report, while to some extent providing a new baseline, is not intended to, and could not, freeze the scale of damages either absolutely or in relative terms as between different categories of loss. May I convey my sincere congratulations to the authors upon the excellent way in which they have performed their task.

Lord Donaldson of Lymington
25 March 1992

Introduction to the Judicial College Guidelines–Twelfth Edition

Since the 11ᵗʰ edition inflation has been relatively modest. The figures in the book have been updated to reflect inflation to the end of April 2013 which, according to the RPI index, was 2.8% since the date which informed the 11ᵗʰ edition. We have rounded the figures, some up and some down, to provide realistic brackets. Judges do not award general damages save in rounded figures. In rounding both up and down we aim to avoid inadvertently generally overstating or understating the impact of inflation.

The editors have taken account of decisions since the preparation of the last edition. Additionally, Chapter 3 now includes a reference to 'post concussion syndrome' and the sections dealing with asbestos related disease have been revised.

In the introduction to the 11ᵗʰ edition we foreshadowed the 10% increase in general damages for pain, suffering and loss of amenity to coincide with the legislative changes introducing the Jackson Reforms. We referred to the decision of the Court of Appeal in *Simmons v Castle* in July 2012, [2012] EWCA Civ 1039. That had suggested that a 10% increase in general damages would apply to all cases decided from 1 April 2013, irrespective of the funding arrangements in place.

In October 2012 the Court of Appeal revisited that conclusion on the application of the Association of British Insurers, [2012] EWCA Civ 1288; [2013] 1 All ER 334. The 10% uplift in general damages recommended by Sir Rupert Jackson was primarily to compensate claimants who were funding litigation through a CFA for the loss of their right to recover the success fee from the defendant. That is the effect of section 44(4) of the Legal Aid, Sentencing and Punishment of Offenders Act 2012. But there are exceptions found in section 44(6). There was a possibility that a claimant would get the increase in general damages and still recover the success fee. The Court of Appeal revisited its earlier conclusion and in paragraph 50 of its judgment said:

> Accordingly, we take this opportunity to declare that, with effect from 1 April 2013, the proper level of general damages in all civil claims for (i) pain and suffering, (ii) loss of amenity, (iii) physical inconvenience and discomfort, (iv) social discredit, or (v) mental distress, will be 10% higher than previously, unless the claimant falls within section 44(6) of LASPO. It therefore follows that, if the action now under appeal had been the subject of a judgment after 1 April 2013, then (unless the claimant had entered into a CFA before that date) the proper award of general damages would be 10% higher than that agreed in this case, namely £22,000 rather than £20,000.

Section 44(6) provides:

> The amendment made by subsection (4) does not prevent a costs order including provision in relation to a success fee payable by a person ("P") under a [CFA] entered into before [1 April 2013] if –
>
> (a) the agreement was entered into specifically for the purpose of the provision to P of advocacy or litigation services in connection with the matter that is the subject of the proceedings in which the costs order is made, or
>
> (b) advocacy or litigation services were provided to P under the agreement in connection with that matter before [1 April 2013].

The simple statement of principle by the Court of Appeal and section 44(6) will undoubtedly be the subject of further consideration in the coming months in the light of the Conditional Fee Agreements Order 2013. In particular the question of how to approach general damages in cases where a CFA for litigation services pre-dates 1 April 2013, but the CFA for advocacy services post-dates it will need to be determined.

This edition contains both the pre and post Jackson reforms figures for ease of reference. At least for the life of this edition practitioners will be constantly dealing with cases falling on both sides of the divide.

No decided case of which we are aware has taken up the challenge which both I and Dame Janet Smith issued in the last edition to rationalise awards for scarring and disfigurement between men and women. So the dual approach survives for the moment. We would be particularly interested to hear how these awards are being dealt with in negotiations leading to settlement.

Having overseen many editions of this work, Andrea Dowsett has passed on responsibility within the Judicial College to Mark Dibben. We are grateful to Andrea for all she has done in support of this work. Comments and suggestions on this edition may be sent to JCPublications@judiciary.gsi.gov.uk Vicky Pittman at Oxford University Press continues gently to keep us on track whilst tolerating a relaxed approach to deadlines.

Ian Burnett
9 July 2013

Note on Multiple Injuries

The assessment of general damages in multiple injury cases can give rise to special difficulty, in particular in determining the extent to which there is any overlap between injuries and how this should be reflected in the overall award. An illustration of such difficulties, and guidance as to the approach to be taken, can be found in the recent Court of Appeal decision in Sadler v Filipiak [2011] EWCA Civ 1728. We can do no better than quote in full paragraph 34 of the judgment of Pitchford LJ in that case:

It is in my judgment always necessary to stand back from the compilation of individual figures, whether assistance has been derived from comparable cases or from the [Judicial College] guideline advice, to consider whether the award for pain, suffering and loss of amenity should be greater than the sum of the parts in order properly to reflect the combined effect of all the injuries upon the injured person's recovering quality of life or, on the contrary, should be smaller than the sum of the parts in order to remove an element of double counting. In some cases, no doubt a minority, no adjustment will be necessary because the total will properly reflect the overall pain, suffering and loss of amenity endured. In others, and probably the majority, an adjustment and occasionally a significant adjustment may be necessary.

1

Injuries Resulting in Death

Fatal accident claims sometimes include an element for pain, suffering and loss of amenity for the period between injury and death. In some circumstances the awards may be high, for example those relating to asbestos exposure or misdiagnosis of cancer. Others follow extensive periods of disability before death supervenes. In such cases reference should be made to the awards for the underlying injuries or condition, suitably adjusted to reflect the fact (if it be the case) that the claimant knows that death is approaching, and the period of suffering.

Yet there are many cases in which a serious injury is followed relatively quickly by death. Factors that inform the level of general damages include the nature and extent of the injury, the claimant's awareness of his impending death, the extent or pain and suffering or, in cases where the claimant is unconscious for all or part of the period, loss of amenity.

		with 10% uplift
(A) FULL AWARENESS	£15,400	£16,940
	to £17,500	to £19,250

Severe burns and lung damage followed by full awareness for a short period and then fluctuating levels of consciousness for between four and five weeks, coupled with intrusive treatment.

		with 10% uplift
(B) FOLLOWED BY UNCONSCIOUSNESS	£7,700 to £10,300	£8,470 to £11,330

Severe burns and lung damage causing excruciating pain but followed by unconsciousness after 3 hours and death two weeks later; or very severe chest and extensive orthopaedic injuries from which recovery was being made, but complications supervened.

(C) IMMEDIATE UNCONSCIOUSNESS/DEATH AFTER SIX WEEKS	£6,200	£6,820

Immediate unconsciousness after injury, and death occurring after six weeks.

(D) IMMEDIATE UNCONSCIOUSNESS/DEATH WITHIN ONE WEEK	£1,000 to £2,050	£1,100 to £2,255

Immediate unconsciousness, or unconsciousness following very shortly after injury, and death occurring within a week.

2

Injuries Involving Paralysis

			with 10% uplift
(a)	**Tetraplegia (also known as Quadriplegia)**	**£238,500 to £297,000**	£262,350 to £326,700

The typical case of tetraplegia attracting an award in the mid-range of this bracket is appropriate for cases in which the injured person is not in physical pain, has full awareness of their disability, has an expectation of life of 25 years or more, has retained powers of speech, sight and hearing but needs help with bodily functions. At the top end of the bracket will be cases where physical pain is present or where there is a significant effect on senses or ability to communicate. Such cases often involve significant brain damage where degree of insight is a relevant factor: see 3(A)(a). Lack of awareness/significantly reduced life expectancy will justify a below average award. Other factors bearing on the award include age, the extent of any residual movement, the degree of independence (if any) whether through the provision of aids/equipment or otherwise, the presence of respiratory issues and depression

with 10% uplift

(b) Paraplegia	**£161,000 to £209,000**	£177,100 to £229,900

The level of the award within the bracket will be affected by the following considerations:

(i)   the presence and extent of pain;

(ii)   the degree of independence;

(iii)   depression;

(iv)   age and life expectancy.

The presence of increasing paralysis or the degree of risk that this will occur, for example, from syringomyelia, might take the case above this bracket, as may the presence of other significant injuries. The former might be the subject of a provisional damages order.

3

Head Injury

This chapter is primarily concerned with injury that produces physiological dysfunction of the brain as a consequence of injury to the head or brain. The clinical severity of brain injury is generally (but not exclusively) classified as mild/moderate/severe by reference to the Glasgow Coma Scale and/or the period of Post-Traumatic Amnesia. The classification will also often involve an analysis of any CT/MRI scanning taken in the aftermath of injury. By contrast the categories in this chapter principally reflect the severity of outcome.

Although at the interface with Psychiatric injury, diagnosed cases of Post-Concussional Syndrome ('PCS') following injury to the head can also be considered within this chapter. Symptoms commonly include headaches, dizziness, and nausea. Permanent symptoms can result, but most cases resolve within two years. Awards should reflect the nature and severity of symptoms rather than any diagnostic label.

(A) Brain Damage

(a) **Very Severe Brain Damage**	£207,250 to £297,000	£227,975 to £326,700

In cases at the top of this bracket the injured person will have a degree of insight. There may be some ability to follow basic commands, recovery of eye opening and return of sleep and waking patterns and postural reflex movement. There will be little, if any, evidence of meaningful response to environment, little or no language function, double incontinence and the need for full-time nursing care.

The level of the award within the bracket will be affected by:

(i)   the degree of insight;

(ii)   life expectancy;

(iii)   the extent of physical limitations.

The top of the bracket will be appropriate only where there is significant effect on the senses and severe physical limitation.

Where there is a persistent vegetative state and/or death occurs very soon after the injuries were suffered and there has been no awareness by the injured person of his or her condition the award will be solely for loss of amenity and will fall substantially below the above bracket.

with 10% uplift

(b) Moderately Severe Brain Damage	**£161,000 to £207,250**	£177,100 to £227,975

The injured person will be very seriously disabled. There will be substantial dependence on others and a need for constant professional and other care. Disabilities may be physical, for example, limb paralysis, or cognitive, with marked impairment of intellect and personality. Cases otherwise within (a) above may fall into this bracket if life expectancy has been greatly reduced. Where there is a risk of associated future development of other severe medical problems such as blindness an award in excess of the bracket would be justified.

The level of the award within the bracket will be affected by the following considerations:

  (i)   the degree of insight;

 (ii)   life expectancy;

(iii)   the extent of physical limitations;

 (iv)   the degree of dependence on others;

  (v)   ability to communicate;

 (vi)   behavioural abnormality;

(vii)   epilepsy or a significant risk of epilepsy (unless a provisional damages order provides for this risk).

(c) Moderate Brain Damage

This category is distinguished from (b) by the fact that the degree of dependence is markedly lower.

with 10% uplift

(i) Cases in which there is moderate to severe intellectual deficit, a personality change, an effect on sight, speech and senses with a significant risk of epilepsy and no prospect of employment.

£110,300 to £161,000

£121,330 to £177,100

(ii) Cases in which there is a moderate to modest intellectual deficit, the ability to work is greatly reduced if not removed and there is some risk of epilepsy (unless a provisional damages order provides for this risk).

£66,600 to £110,300

£73,260 to £121,330

(iii) Cases in which concentration and memory are affected, the ability to work is reduced, where there is a small risk of epilepsy and any dependence on others is very limited.

£31,650 to £66,600

£34,815 to £73,260

(d) Less Severe Brain Damage

£11,250 to £31,600

£12,375 to £34,760

In these cases the injured person will have made a good recovery and will be able to take part in normal social life and to return to work. There may not have been a restoration of all normal functions so there may still be persisting problems such as poor concentration and memory or disinhibition of mood, which may interfere with lifestyle, leisure activities and future work prospects. At the top of this bracket there may be a small risk of epilepsy.

The level of the award within the bracket will be affected by:

(i) the extent and severity of the initial injury;

(ii) the extent of any continuing, and possibly permanent, disability;

(iii) the extent of any personality change;

(iv) depression.

		with 10% uplift
(e) Minor Brain or Head Injury	**£1,625 to £9,400**	£1,788 to £10,340

In these cases brain damage, if any, will have been minimal.

The level of the award will be affected by the following considerations:

(i) the severity of the initial injury;

(ii) the period taken to recover from any symptoms;

(iii) the extent of continuing symptoms;

(iv) the presence or absence of headaches.

The bottom of the bracket will reflect full recovery within a few weeks.

(B) EPILEPSY

(a) Established Grand Mal	**£75,000 to £110,300**	£82,500 to £121,330

		with 10% uplift

(b) Established Petit Mal   £40,300 to £96,300   £44,330 to £105,930

The level of the award within these brackets will be affected by the following factors:

   (i) whether attacks are successfully controlled by medication and the extent to which the need for medication is likely to persist;

   (ii) the extent to which the appreciation of life is blunted by such medication;

   (iii) the effect on working and/or social life;

   (iv) the existence of associated behavioural problems;

   (v) the prognosis.

(c) Other Epileptic Conditions   £7,800 to £19,300   £8,580 to £21,230

Cases where there are one or two discrete epileptic episodes, or a temporary resurgence of epilepsy, but there is no risk of further recurrence beyond that applicable to the population at large. The level of the award within the bracket will be affected by the extent of any consequences of the attacks on, for example, education, sporting activities, working and social life, and their duration.

4

Psychiatric and Psychological Damage

This chapter covers those cases where there is a recognisable psychiatric injury. In part (A) of this chapter some of the brackets contain an element of compensation for post-traumatic stress disorder. This is of course not a universal feature of cases of psychiatric injury and hence a number of the awards upon which the brackets are based did not reflect it. Where it does figure any award will tend towards the upper end of the bracket. Cases where post-traumatic stress disorder is the sole psychiatric condition are dealt with in part (B) of this chapter. Where cases arise out of sexual and/or physical abuse in breach of parental, family or other trust, involving victims who are young and/or vulnerable, awards will tend to be at the upper end of the relevant bracket to take into account (A)(vii) below.

Where the psychiatric injury arises out of the death of a close relative, e.g. a child, spouse or parent, awards will tend to fall into (A)(c) below unless the long-term prognosis is especially poor when an award within (A)(b) may be appropriate. Similarly, where the death causes post-traumatic stress disorder awards will tend to fall into (B)(b) or (c) below.

(A) PSYCHIATRIC DAMAGE GENERALLY

The factors to be taken into account in valuing claims of this nature are as follows:

(i) the injured person's ability to cope with life and work;

(ii) the effect on the injured person's relationships with family, friends and those with whom he or she comes into contact;

(iii) the extent to which treatment would be successful;

(iv) future vulnerability;

(v) prognosis;

(vi) whether medical help has been sought;

(vii) Claims relating to sexual and physical abuse usually include a significant aspect of psychiatric or psychological damage. The brackets discussed in this chapter provide a useful starting point in the assessment of general damages in such cases. It should not be forgotten, however, that this aspect of the injury is likely to form only part of the injury for which damages will be awarded. Many cases include physical or sexual abuse and injury. Others have an element of false imprisonment. The fact of an abuse of trust is relevant to the award of damages. A further feature, which distinguishes these cases from most involving psychiatric damage, is that there may have been a long period during which the effects of the abuse were undiagnosed, untreated, unrecognised or even denied. Aggravated damages may be appropriate.

		with 10% uplift
(a) Severe	**£40,300 to £85,000**	£44,330 to £93,500

In these cases the injured person will have marked problems with respect to factors (i) to (iv) above and the prognosis will be very poor.

(b) Moderately Severe	**£14,000 to £40,300**	£15,400 to £44,330

In these cases there will be significant problems associated with factors (i) to (iv) above but the prognosis will be much more optimistic than in (a) above. While there are awards which support both extremes of this bracket, the majority are somewhere near the middle of the bracket. Cases of work-related stress resulting in a permanent or long-standing disability preventing a return to comparable employment would appear to come within this category.

(c) Moderate	**£4,300 to £14,000**	£4,730 to £15,400

While there may have been the sort of problems associated with factors (i) to (iv) above there will have been marked improvement by trial and the prognosis will be good.

		with 10% uplift
(d) Less Severe	**£1,125 to £4,300**	£1,238 to £4,730

The level of the award will take into consideration the length of the period of disability and the extent to which daily activities and sleep were affected. Cases falling short of a specific phobia or disorder such as travel anxiety when associated with minor physical symptoms may be found in the Minor Injuries chapter.

(B) POST-TRAUMATIC STRESS DISORDER

Cases within this category are exclusively those where there is a specific diagnosis of a reactive psychiatric disorder in which characteristic symptoms are displayed following a psychologically distressing event which causes intense fear, helplessness and horror. The guidelines below have been compiled by reference to cases which variously reflect the criteria established in the 4th edition of *Diagnostic and Statistical Manual of Mental Disorders* (DSM-IV-TR). The symptoms affect basic functions such as breathing, pulse rate and bowel and/or bladder control. They also involve persistent re-experience of the relevant event, difficulty in controlling temper, in concentrating and sleeping, and exaggerated startle response.

(a) Severe	**£44,000 to £74,000**	£48,400 to £81,400

Such cases will involve permanent effects which prevent the injured person from working at all or at least from functioning at anything approaching the pre-trauma level. All aspects of the life of the injured person will be badly affected.

		with 10% uplift
(b) **Moderately Severe**	**£17,000** **to £44,000**	£18,700 to £48,400

This category is distinct from (a) above because of the better prognosis which will be for some recovery with professional help. However, the effects are still likely to cause significant disability for the foreseeable future. While there are awards which support both extremes of this bracket, the majority are between £21,000 and £27,000.

(c) **Moderate**	**£6,000** **to £17,000**	£6,600 to £18,700

In these cases the injured person will have largely recovered and any continuing effects will not be grossly disabling.

(d) **Less Severe**	**£2,900** **to £6,000**	£3,190 to £6,600

In these cases a virtually full recovery will have been made within one to two years and only minor symptoms will persist over any longer period.

5

Injuries Affecting the Senses

(A) Injuries Affecting Sight

			with 10% uplift
(a)	**Total Blindness and Deafness**	**In the region of £297,000**	In the region of £326,700

Such cases must be considered as ranking with the most devastating injuries.

(b)	**Total Blindness**	**In the region of £197,500**	In the region of £217,250

(c) **Loss of Sight in One Eye with Reduced Vision in the Remaining Eye**

(i)	Where there is serious risk of further deterioration in the remaining eye, going beyond some risk of sympathetic ophthalmia.	**£70,500 to £132,000**	£77,550 to £145,200
(ii)	Where there is reduced vision in the remaining eye and/or additional problems such as double vision.	**£47,000 to £78,000**	£51,700 to £85,800

(d)	**Total Loss of One Eye**	**£40,300 to £48,200**	£44,330 to £53,020

The level of the award within the bracket will depend on age and cosmetic effect.

			with 10% uplift
(e)	**Complete Loss of Sight in One Eye**	**£36,200 to £40,300**	£39,820 to £44,330

This award takes account of some risk of sympathetic ophthalmia. The upper end of the bracket is appropriate where there is scarring in the region of the eye which is not sufficiently serious to merit a separate award.

(f)	Cases of serious but incomplete loss of vision in one eye without significant risk of loss or reduction of vision in the remaining eye, or where there is constant double vision.	**£17,400 to £28,750**	£19,140 to £31,625

(g)	Minor but permanent impairment of vision in one or both eyes, including cases where there is some double vision, which may not be constant.	**£6,700 to £15,400**	£7,370 to £16,940

(h)	**Minor Eye Injuries**	**£2,900 to £6,400**	£3,190 to £7,040

In this bracket fall cases of minor injuries, such as being struck in the eye, exposure to fumes including smoke, or being splashed by liquids, causing initial pain and some temporary interference with vision.

(i)	**Transient Eye Injuries**	**£1,620 to £2,900**	£1,782 to £3,190

In these cases the injured person will have recovered completely within a few weeks.

(B) DEAFNESS/TINNITUS

The word 'deafness' is used to embrace total and partial hearing loss. In assessing awards for hearing loss regard must be had to the following:

(i) whether the injury is one that has an immediate effect, allowing no opportunity to adapt, or whether it occurred over a period of time, as in noise exposure cases;

(ii) whether the injury or disability is one which the injured person suffered at an early age so that it has had or will have an effect on his or her speech (and will be suffered for a longer period), or is one that is suffered in later life;

(iii) whether the injury or disability affects balance;

(iv) in cases of noise-induced hearing loss (NIHL) age is of particular relevance as noted in paragraph (d) below;

(v) tinnitus may be suffered alone, rather than associated with NIHL.

Note also that the cases which form the basis of these brackets were decided before recent advances in medical science, such as cochlear implants which can in some cases restore total deafness to almost full hearing when worn.

		with 10% uplift
	£80,600	£88,660
(a) Total Deafness and Loss of Speech	**to £103,250**	to £113,575

Such cases arise, for example, where deafness has occurred at an early age (for example, rubella infection) so as to prevent or seriously to affect the development of normal speech.

(b) Total Deafness	£66,650	£73,315
	to £80,600	to £88,660

The lower end of the bracket is appropriate for cases where there is no speech deficit or tinnitus. The higher end is appropriate for cases involving both of these.

(c) Total Loss of Hearing in One Ear	£23,000	£25,300
	to £33,500	to £36,850

Cases will tend towards the higher end of the bracket where there are associated problems, such as tinnitus, dizziness or headaches.

(d) Partial Hearing Loss and/or Tinnitus

This category covers the bulk of deafness cases which usually result from exposure to noise over a prolonged period. The disability is not to be judged simply by the degree of hearing loss; there is often a degree of tinnitus present. Age is particularly relevant because impairment of hearing affects most people in the fullness of time and impacts both upon causation and upon valuation.

			with 10% uplift
(i)	Severe tinnitus and hearing loss.	**£21,800 to £33,500**	£23,980 to £36,850
(ii)	Moderate tinnitus and hearing loss or moderate to severe tinnitus or hearing loss alone.	**£11,000 to £21,800**	£12,100 to £23,980
(iii)	Mild tinnitus with some hearing loss.	**£9,250 to £11,000**	£10,175 to £12,100
(iv)	Slight or occasional tinnitus with slight hearing loss.	**£5,400 to £9,250**	£5,940 to £10,175
(v)	Slight hearing loss without tinnitus or slight tinnitus without hearing loss.	**Up to £5,150**	Up to £5,665

(C) IMPAIRMENT OF TASTE AND SMELL

It is rare to find an injury which causes loss of taste and/or smell alone. Such symptoms are usually associated with brain injury or infection, in which case regard should be had to the guidelines for those injuries.

(a)	**Total Loss of Taste and Smell**	**In the region of £28,750**	In the region of £31,625

(b)	**Total Loss of Smell and Significant Loss of Taste**	**£24,200 to £28,750**	£26,620 to £31,625

It must be remembered that in nearly all cases of loss of smell there is some

impairment of taste. Such cases fall into
the next bracket.

			with 10% uplift
(c)	**Loss of Smell**	**£18,350 to £24,200**	£20,185 to £26,620
(d)	**Loss of Taste**	**£14,100 to £18,350**	£15,510 to £20,185

6

Injuries to Internal Organs

(A) CHEST INJURIES

This is a specially difficult area because the majority of awards relate to industrial *disease* (see (B) below) as distinct from traumatic *injury*. Cases of traumatic damage to, or loss of, a lung are comparatively rare and the range is very wide.

The levels of awards within the brackets set out below will be affected by:

(i) age and gender;

(ii) scarring;

(iii) the effect on the capacity to work and enjoy life;

(iv) the effect on life expectancy.

			with 10% uplift
(a)	The worst type of case will be of total removal of one lung and/or serious heart damage with serious and prolonged pain and suffering and permanent significant scarring.	**£74,000 to £110,300**	£81,400 to £121,330
(b)	Traumatic injury to chest, lung(s) and/orheart causing permanent damage, impairment of function, physical disability and reduction of life expectancy.	**£48,250 to £74,000**	£53,075 to £81,400

			with 10% uplift
(c)	Damage to chest and lung(s) causing some continuing disability.	£23,000 to £40,300	£25,300 to £44,330
(d)	A relatively simple injury (such as a single penetrating wound) causing some permanent damage to tissue but with no significant long-term effect on lung function.	£9,250 to £13,200	£10,175 to £14,520
(e)	Toxic fume/smoke inhalation, leaving some residual damage, not serious enough to interfere permanently with lung function.	£3,900 to £9,250	£4,290 to £10,175
(f)	Injuries leading to collapsed lungs from which a full and uncomplicated recovery is made.	£1,600 to £3,900	£1,760 to £4,290
(g)	Fractures of ribs or soft tissue injuries causing serious pain and disability over a period of weeks only.	Up to £2,900	Up to £3,190

(B) Lung Disease

The level of the appropriate award for lung disease necessarily, and often principally, reflects the prognosis for what is frequently a worsening condition and/or the risk of the development of secondary sequelae.

Most of the reported cases are of asbestos-related disease (as to which see (C) below) but, save for asthma (which is also dealt with separately in (D) below), the brackets set out are intended to encompass all other lung disease cases irrespective of causation. In many cases falling under this head provisional awards will be appropriate. At the upper end of the range where serious disabling consequences will already be present and the prognosis is likely to be relatively clear such an award may not be appropriate. Furthermore, in some cases awards may be enhanced where classifiable psychiatric illness is present.

			with 10% uplift
(a)	For a young person with serious disability where there is a probability of progressive worsening leading to premature death.	£74,000 to £100,000	£81,400 to £110,000
(b)	Lung cancer (typically in an older person) causing severe pain and impairment both of function and of quality of life. Practitioners may find some of the factors set out in C(a) useful in determining variations within the bracket.	£51,500 to £71,500	£56,650 to £78,650
(c)	Disease, e.g., emphysema, causing significant and worsening lung function and impairment of breathing, prolonged and frequent coughing, sleep disturbance and restriction of physical activity and employment.	£40,250 to £51,500	£44,275 to £56,650
(d)	Breathing difficulties (short of disabling breathlessness) requiring fairly frequent use of an inhaler; where there is inability to tolerate a smoky environment and an uncertain prognosis but already significant effect on social and working life.	£23,000 to £40,300	£25,300 to £44,330
(e)	Bronchitis and wheezing not causing serious symptoms; little or no serious or permanent effect on working or social life; varying levels of anxiety about the future.	£15,300 to £23,000	£16,830 to £25,300
(f)	Some slight breathlessness with no effect on working life and the likelihood of substantial and permanent recovery within a	£7,800 to £15,300	£8,580 to £16,830

few years of the exposure to the cause or
the aggravation of an existing condition.

			with 10% uplift
(g)	Provisional awards for cases otherwise falling within (f), or the least serious cases within (e) where the provisional award excludes any risk of malignancy.	£3,900 to £7,800	£4,290 to £8,580
(h)	Temporary aggravation of bronchitis or other chest problems resolving within a very few months.	£1,620 to £3,900	£1,782 to £4,290

(C) ASBESTOS-RELATED DISEASE

Mesothelioma, lung cancer and asbestosis
are the most serious of these. Mesothelioma
is typically of shorter duration than
either of the other two and often proves
fatal within a matter of months from first
diagnosis. Lung cancer and asbestosis
are likely to have a fatal outcome but the
symptoms often endure for several years.
Most of the recent reported cases concern
mesothelioma. Cases of lung cancer and
asbestosis may result in similar levels of
symptoms to mesothelioma, which may
justify awards in excess of the suggested
upper brackets for those conditions.

(a)	Mesothelioma causing severe pain and impairment of both function and quality of life. This may be of the pleura (the lung lining) or of the peritoneum (the lining of the abdominal cavity); the latter being typically more painful. There are a large number of factors which will affect the level of award within the bracket. These include but are not limited to duration of	£51,500 to £92,500	£56,650 to £101,750

pain and suffering, extent and effects of invasive investigations, extent and effects of radical surgery, chemotherapy and radiotherapy, whether the mesothelioma is peritoneal or pleural, the extent to which the tumour has spread to encase the lungs and where other organs become involved causing additional pain and/or breathlessness, the level of the symptoms, domestic circumstances, age, level of activity and previous state of health.

		with 10% uplift
(b) Lung cancer, again a disease proving fatal in most cases, the symptoms of which may not be as painful as those of mesothelioma, but more protracted. As with (B)(b) above, practitioners may find some of the factors in C(a) above useful in determining variations within the bracket.	£51,500 to £71,500	£56,650 to £78,650
(c) Asbestosis and pleural thickening—where the level of disability attributable to asbestos will be in excess of 10% causing progressive symptoms of breathlessness by reducing lung function. Awards at the lower end of the bracket will be applicable where the condition is relatively static. Higher awards will be applicable where the condition has progressed or is likely to progress to cause more severe breathlessness. Awards at the top end of the bracket will be applicable where mobility and quality of life has or is likely to become significantly impaired and/or life expectancy significantly reduced. This is a wide bracket and the extent of respiratory disability will be highly significant with disabilities of 10-30% being at the lower end, 30-50% in the middle and in excess of 50% at the higher end.	£28,250 to £77,800	£31,075 to £85,580

		with 10% uplift
(d) Asbestosis and pleural thickening—where the level of respiratory disability/lung function impairment attributable to asbestos is 1–10%.	**£11,100 to £28,250**	£12,210 to £31,075

The level of award will influenced by whether it is to be final or on a provisional basis.

(D) ASTHMA

(a) Severe and permanent disabling asthma, causing prolonged and regular coughing, disturbance of sleep, severe impairment of physical activity and enjoyment of life and where employment prospects, if any, are grossly restricted.	**£31,650 to £48,250**	£34,815 to £53,075
(b) Chronic asthma causing breathing difficulties, the need to use an inhaler from time to time and restriction of employment prospects, with uncertain prognosis.	**£19,300 to £31,600**	£21,230 to £34,760
(c) Bronchitis and wheezing, affecting working or social life, with the likelihood of substantial recovery within a few years of the exposure to the cause.	**£14,100 to £19,300**	£15,510 to £21,230
(d) Relatively mild asthma-like symptoms often resulting, for instance, from exposure to harmful irritating vapour.	**£7,800 to £14,100**	£8,580 to £15,510
(e) Mild asthma, bronchitis, colds and chest problems (usually resulting from unfit housing or similar exposure, particularly in cases of young children) treated by a	**Up to £3,800**	Up to £4,180

general practitioner and resolving within
a few months.

(E) Reproductive System: Male

with 10% uplift

(a) Total Loss of Reproductive Organs	**In excess of £113,000**	In excess of £124,300

(b) Impotence

    (i) Total impotence and loss of sexual function and sterility in the case of a young man. — **In the region of £109,000** — In the region of £119,900

    The level of the award will depend on:

    (1) age;

    (2) psychological reaction and the effect on social and domestic life.

    (ii) Impotence which is likely to be permanent, in the case of a middle-aged man with children. — **£31,600 to £57,600** — £34,760 to £63,360

(c) Cases of sterility usually fall into one of two categories: surgical, chemical and disease cases (which involve no traumatic injury or scarring) and traumatic injuries (frequently caused by assaults) which are often aggravated by scarring.

    (i) The most serious cases merit awards up to — **£103,250** — £113,575

    (ii) The bottom of the range is the case of the much older man and merits an award of about — **£13,800** — £15,180

			with 10% uplift
(d)	An uncomplicated case of sterility without impotence and without any aggravating features for a young man without children.	**£41,250 to £52,400**	£45,375 to £57,640
(e)	A similar case but involving a family man who might have intended to have more children.	**£17,400 to £23,000**	£19,140 to £25,300
(f)	Cases where the sterility amounts to little more than an 'insult'.	**In the region of £4,900**	In the region of £5,390

(F) REPRODUCTIVE SYSTEM: FEMALE

The level of awards in this area will typically depend on:

(i) whether or not the affected woman already has children and/or whether the intended family was complete;

(ii) scarring;

(iii) depression or psychological scarring;

(iv) whether a foetus was aborted.

(a)	Infertility whether by reason of injury or disease, with severe depression and anxiety, pain and scarring.	**£84,500 to £124,500**	£92,950 to £136,950
(b)	Infertility without any medical complication and where the injured person already has children. The upper end of the bracket is appropriate in cases where there is significant psychological damage.	**£13,200 to £27,000**	£14,520 to £29,700

with 10% uplift

(c) Infertility where the injured person would not have had children in any event (for example, because of age). — **£4,900 to £9,250** — £5,390 to £10,175

(d) Failed sterilisation leading to unwanted pregnancy where there is no serious psychological impact or depression. — **In the region of £7,500** — In the region of £8,250

(G) DIGESTIVE SYSTEM

The risk of associated damage to the reproductive organs is frequently encountered in cases of this nature and requires separate consideration.

(a) Damage Resulting from Traumatic Injury

(i) Severe damage with continuing pain and discomfort. — **£31,600 to £45,500** — £34,760 to £50,050

(ii) Serious non-penetrating injury causing long-standing or permanent complications, for example, severe indigestion, aggravated by physical strain. — **£12,350 to £20,400** — £13,585 to £22,440

(iii) Penetrating stab wounds or industrial laceration or serious seat-belt pressure cases. — **£4,900 to £9,250** — £5,390 to £10,175

(b) Illness/Damage Resulting from Non-traumatic Injury, e.g. Food Poisoning

There will be a marked distinction between those, comparatively rare, cases having a long-standing or even permanent effect on quality of life and those in which the only continuing symptoms may be allergy to specific foods and the attendant risk of short-term illness.

		with 10% uplift
(i)	Severe toxicosis causing serious acute pain, vomiting, diarrhoea and fever, requiring hospital admission for some days or weeks and some continuing incontinence, haemorrhoids and irritable bowel syndrome, having a significant impact on ability to work and enjoyment of life.	**£28,250 to £38,600**	£31,075 to £42,460
(ii)	Serious but short-lived food poisoning, diarrhoea and vomiting diminishing over two to four weeks with some remaining discomfort and disturbance of bowel function and impact on sex life and enjoyment of food over a few years. Any such symptoms having these consequences and lasting for longer, even indefinitely, are likely to merit an award between the top of this bracket and the bottom of the bracket in (i) above.	**£7,000 to £14,100**	£7,700 to £15,510
(iii)	Food poisoning causing significant discomfort, stomach cramps, alteration of bowel function and fatigue. Hospital admission for some days with symptoms lasting for a few weeks but complete recovery within a year or two.	**£2,900 to £7,000**	£3,190 to £7,700
(iv)	Varying degrees of disabling pain, cramps and diarrhoea continuing for some days or weeks.	**£670 to £2,900**	£737 to £3,190

(H) Kidney

with 10% uplift

(a)	Serious and permanent damage to or loss of both kidneys.	**£124,500 to £154,500**	£136,950 to £169,950
(b)	Where there is a significant risk of future urinary tract infection or other total loss of natural kidney function.	**Up to £47,000**	Up to £51,700
	Such cases will invariably carry with them substantial future medical expenses, which in this field are particularly high.		
(c)	Loss of one kidney with no damage to the other.	**£22,600 to £33,000**	£24,860 to £36,300

(I) Bowels

(a)	Total loss of natural function and dependence on colostomy, depending on age.	**Up to £110,300**	Up to £121,330
(b)	Severe abdominal injury causing impairment of function and often necessitating temporary colostomy (leaving disfiguring scars) and/or restriction on employment and on diet.	**£32,750 to £51,250**	£36,025 to £56,375
(c)	Penetrating injuries causing some permanent damage but with an eventual return to natural function and control.	**£9,250 to £18,000**	£10,175 to £19,800

(J) Bladder

It is perhaps surprising that awards in cases of loss of bladder function have often been higher than awards for injury to the bowels. This is probably because bladder injuries frequently result from carcinogenic exposure.

			with 10% uplift
(a)	Complete loss of function and control.	**Up to £103,250**	Up to £113,575
(b)	Serious impairment of control with some pain and incontinence.	**£47,000 to £58,750**	£51,700 to £64,625
(c)	Where there has been almost a complete recovery but some fairly long-term interference with natural function.	**£17,200 to £23,000**	£18,920 to £25,300

The cancer risk cases still occupy a special category and can properly attract awards at the top of the ranges even where natural function continues for the time being. If the prognosis is firm and reliable the award will reflect any loss of life expectancy, the level of continuing pain and suffering and most significantly the extent to which the injured person has to live with the knowledge of the consequences which his or her death will have for others. The appropriate award for the middle-aged family man or woman whose life expectancy is reduced by 15 or 20 years is £38,000 to £56,000.

(K) SPLEEN

(a)	Loss of spleen where there is continuing risk of internal infection and disorders due to the damage to the immune system.	**£15,300 to £19,300**	£16,830 to £21,230
(b)	Where the above risks are not present or are minimal.	**£3,200 to £6,350**	£3,520 to £6,985

(L) Hernia

with 10% uplift

(a)	Continuing pain and/or limitation on physical activities, sport or employment, after repair.	**£11,000 to £17,750**	£12,100 to £19,525
(b)	Direct (where there was no pre-existing weakness) inguinal hernia, with some risk of recurrence, after repair.	**£5,150 to £6,700**	£5,665 to £7,370
(c)	Uncomplicated indirect inguinal hernia, possibly repaired, and with no other associated abdominal injury or damage.	**£2,500 to £5,300**	£2,750 to £5,830

7

Orthopaedic Injuries

(A) NECK INJURIES

There is a very wide range of neck injuries.
Many are found in conjunction with
back and shoulder problems. At the very
bottom end of neck and back injuries,
further guidance may be obtained
from the Minor Injuries chapter in the
Guidelines.

(a) Severe

			with 10% uplift
(i)	Neck injury associated with incomplete paraplegia or resulting in permanent spastic quadriparesis or where the injured person, despite wearing a collar 24 hours a day for a period of years, still has little or no movement in the neck and suffers severe headaches which have proved intractable.	**In the region of £109,000**	In the region of £119,900
(ii)	Injuries, usually involving serious fractures or damage to discs in the cervical spine, which give rise to disabilities which fall short of those in (a)(i) above but which are of considerable severity; for example, permanent damage to the brachial plexus or substantial loss of movement in the neck and loss of function in one or more limbs.	**£48,250 to £96,250**	£53,075 to £105,875

35

with 10% uplift

(iii) Injuries causing fractures or dislocations or severe damage to soft tissues and/or ruptured tendons that lead to chronic conditions and significant disability of a permanent nature. The precise award depends on the length of time during which the most serious symptoms are ameliorated, the extent of the treatment required and on the prognosis.	**£33,400 to £41,150**	£36,740 to £45,265

(b) Moderate

(i) Injuries such as fractures or dislocations which cause severe immediate symptoms and which may necessitate spinal fusion. This bracket will also include chronic conditions, usually involving referred symptoms to other parts of the anatomy or serious soft tissue injuries to the neck and back combined. They leave markedly impaired function or vulnerability to further trauma, and limitation of activities.	**£18,350 to £28,300**	£20,185 to £31,130
(ii) Cases involving soft tissue or wrenching-type injury and disc lesion of the more severe type resulting in cervical spondylosis, serious limitation of movement, permanent or recurring pain, stiffness or discomfort and the possible need for further surgery or increased vulnerability to further trauma. This bracket will also include injuries which may have accelerated and/or exacerbated a pre-existing condition over a prolonged period of time, usually by five years or more.	**£10,100 to £18,350**	£11,110 to £20,185

		with 10% uplift
(iii) Injuries which may have accelerated and/or exacerbated a pre-existing condition over a shorter period of time, usually less than five years. This bracket will also apply to moderate soft tissue injuries where the period of recovery has been fairly protracted and where there remains an increased vulnerability to further trauma.	**£5,800 to £10,100**	£6,380 to £11,110

(c) Minor

This bracket includes minor soft tissue injuries. Whilst the duration of symptoms will always be important, the level of award will also be influenced by factors such as:

- the severity of the neck injury;
- the intensity of pain experienced and the consistency of symptoms;
- the presence of additional symptoms in the back and/or shoulder and/or referred headaches;
- the impact of the symptoms on the injured person's ability to function in everyday life and engage in social/recreational activities;
- the impact of the injuries on the injured person's ability to work;
- the extent of any treatment required;
- the need to take medication to control symptoms of pain and discomfort.

(i) Where a full recovery takes place within a period of about one to two years. This bracket will also apply to short-term acceleration and/	**In the region of £3,200 to £5,800**	In the region of £3,520 to £6,380

or exacerbation injuries, usually
between one to two years.

with 10% uplift

(ii) Where a full recovery takes place
within a period of several months
and a year. This bracket will also
apply to very short-term acceleration and/or exacerbation injuries,
usually less than one year.

In the region In the region
of £1,550 of £1,705
to £3,200 to £3,520

(iii) Where a full recovery is made within
a period of a few days, a few weeks or
a few months.

A few A few
hundred hundred
pounds to pounds to
£1,550 £1,705

(B) BACK INJURIES

(a) Severe

(i) Cases of the most severe injury
involving damage to the spinal cord
and nerve roots, leading to a combination of very serious consequences
not normally found in cases of back
injury. There will be severe pain and
disability with a combination of
incomplete paralysis and significantly impaired bladder, bowel and
sexual function.

£67,000 £73,700
to £118,300 to £130,130

(ii) Cases which have special features taking them outside any lower bracket
applicable to orthopaedic injury
to the back. Such features include
nerve root damage with associated
loss of sensation, impaired mobility,
impaired bladder and bowel function, sexual difficulties and unsightly
scarring.

£54,500 £59,950
to £65,000 to £71,500

		with 10% uplift
(iii) Cases of disc lesions or fractures of discs or of vertebral bodies or soft tissue injuries leading to chronic conditions where, despite treatment (usually involving surgery), there remain disabilities such as continuing severe pain and discomfort, impaired agility, impaired sexual function, depression, personality change, alcoholism, unemployability and the risk of arthritis.	**£28,500 to £51,250**	£31,350 to £56,375

(b) Moderate

(i) Cases where any residual disability is of less severity than that in (a)(iii) above. The bracket contains a wide variety of injuries. Examples are a case of a compression/crush fracture of the lumbar vertebrae where there is a substantial risk of osteoarthritis and constant pain and discomfort; that of a traumatic spondylolisthesis with continuous pain and a probability that spinal fusion will be necessary; a prolapsed intervertebral disc requiring surgery or damage to an intervertebral disc with nerve root irritation and reduced mobility.	**£20,400 to £28,500**	£22,440 to £31,350
(ii) Many frequently encountered injuries to the back such as disturbance of ligaments and muscles giving rise to backache, soft tissue injuries resulting in a prolonged acceleration and/or exacerbation of a pre-existing back condition, usually by five years or more, or prolapsed discs necessitating laminectomy or resulting in	**£9,200 to £20,400**	£10,120 to £22,440

repeated relapses. The precise figure will depend upon a number of
factors including the severity of the
original injury, the degree of pain
experienced, the extent of any treatment required in the past or in the
future, the impact of the symptoms
on the injured person's ability to
function in everyday life and engage
in social/recreational activities and
the prognosis for the future.

(c) **Minor**

This bracket includes less serious strains,
sprains, disc prolapses and soft tissue
injuries. As with minor neck injuries,
whilst the duration of symptoms will
always be important, the level of award
will also be influenced by factors such as:

- the severity of the original injury;
- the degree of pain experienced and the
  consistency of symptoms;
- the presence of any additional symptoms in other parts of the anatomy;
- the impact of the symptoms on the
  injured person's ability to function in
  everyday life and engage in social/recre-
  ational activities;
- the impact of the injuries on the injured
  person's ability to work;
- the extent of any treatment required;
- the need to take medication to control
  symptoms of pain and discomfort.

		with 10% uplift
(i) Where a full recovery or a recovery to nuisance level takes place without surgery within about two to five years. This bracket will also apply	In the region of £5,800 to £9,200	In the region of £6,380 to £10,120

		with 10% uplift
to shorter term acceleration and/ or exacerbation injuries, usually between two to five years.		
(ii) Where a full recovery takes place without surgery within a period of several months and two years. This bracket will also apply to very short-term acceleration and/or exacerbation injuries, usually less than two years.	**In the region of £1,550 to £5,800**	In the region of £1,705 to £6,380
(iii) Where a full recovery is made within a period of a few days, or a few weeks or a few months.	**A few hundred pounds to £1,550**	A few hundred pounds to £1,705

(C) Shoulder Injuries

(a) **Severe**	**£14,100 to £35,300**	£15,510 to £38,830

Often associated with neck injuries and involving damage to the brachial plexus (see (A)(a)(ii)) resulting in significant disability. Serious brachial plexus injuries causing significant neck and/or arm symptoms should be assessed under brackets (A)(a)(ii) or (F)(a).

(b) **Serious**	**£9,400 to £14,100**	£10,340 to £15,510

Dislocation of the shoulder and damage to the lower part of the brachial plexus causing pain in shoulder and neck, aching in elbow, sensory symptoms in the forearm and hand, and weakness of grip or a fractured humerus leading to restricted shoulder movement. Cases of rotator cuff injury with persisting symptoms after surgery will usually fall within this bracket, as will cases of soft tissue injury where intrusive symptoms will be permanent.

		with 10% uplift
(c) **Moderate**	£5,800 to £9,400	£6,380 to £10,340

Frozen shoulder with limitation of movement and discomfort with symptoms persisting for about two years. Also soft tissue injuries with more than minimal symptoms persisting after two years but not permanent.

(d) **Minor**

Soft tissue injury to shoulder with considerable pain but almost complete recovery:

(i) in less than two years;	£3,200 to £5,800	£3,520 to £6,380
(ii) within a year.	Up to £3,200	Up to £3,520

(e) **Fracture of Clavicle**	£3,800 to £9,000	£4,180 to £9,900

The level of the award will depend on extent of fracture, level of disability, residual symptoms, and whether temporary or permanent, and whether union is anatomically displaced. Unusually serious cases may exceed this bracket and regard may be had to bracket (C)(b) above.

(D) INJURIES TO THE PELVIS AND HIPS

The most serious of injuries to the pelvis and hip can be as devastating as a leg amputation and accordingly will attract a similar award of damages.

(a) Severe

			with 10% uplift
(i)	Extensive fractures of the pelvis involving, for example, dislocation of a low back joint and a ruptured bladder, or a hip injury resulting in spondylolisthesis of a low back joint with intolerable pain and necessitating spinal fusion. Inevitably there will be substantial residual disabilities such as a complicated arthrodesis with resulting lack of bladder and bowel control, sexual dysfunction or hip deformity making the use of a calliper essential; or may present difficulties for natural delivery.	**£57,600 to £96,250**	£63,360 to £105,875
(ii)	Injuries only a little less severe than in (a)(i) above but with particular distinguishing features lifting them above any lower bracket. Examples are: (a) fracture dislocation of the pelvis involving both ischial and pubic rami and resulting in impotence; or (b) traumatic myositis ossificans with formation of ectopic bone around the hip.	**£45,500 to £57,600**	£50,050 to £63,360
(iii)	Many injuries fall within this bracket: a fracture of the acetabulum leading to degenerative changes and leg instability requiring an osteotomy	**£28,750 to £38,600**	£31,625 to £42,460

and the likelihood of hip replacement surgery in the future; the fracture of an arthritic femur or hip necessitating hip replacement; or a fracture resulting in a hip replacement which is only partially successful so that there is a clear risk of the need for revision surgery.

(b) Moderate

with 10% uplift

(i) Significant injury to the pelvis or hip but any permanent disability is not major and any future risk not great. | **£19,550 to £28,750** | £21,505 to £31,625

(ii) These cases may involve hip replacement or other surgery. Where it has been carried out wholly successfully the award will tend to the top of the bracket, but the bracket also includes cases where hip replacement may be necessary in the foreseeable future or where there are more than minimal ongoing symptoms. | **£9,250 to £19,550** | £10,175 to £21,505

(c) Lesser Injuries

(i) Cases where despite significant injury there is little or no residual disability. Where there has been a complete recovery within two years, the award is unlikely to exceed £5,650 (£6,215 accounting for 10% uplift). | **£2,900 to £9,250** | £3,190 to £10,175

(ii) Minor soft tissue injuries with complete recovery. | **Up to £2,900** | Up to £3,190

(E) AMPUTATION OF ARMS

The value of any amputation injury depends upon:

(i) whether the amputation is above or below the elbow. The loss of the additional joint adds greatly to the disability;

(ii) the extent to which prosthetics can restore function;

(iii) whether or not the amputation was of the dominant arm;

(iv) the intensity of any phantom pains;

(v) the claimant's age;

(vi) the effect on work, domestic and social life.

		with 10% uplift
(a) **Loss of Both Arms**	**£177,000 to £220,500**	**£194,700 to £242,550**

The effect of such an injury is to reduce a person with full awareness to a state of considerable helplessness.

(b) **Loss of One Arm**

(i) Arm Amputated at the Shoulder	**Not less than £100,800**	Not less than £110,880
(ii) Above-elbow Amputation	**£80,600 to £96,250**	£88,660 to £105,875

A shorter stump may create difficulties in the use of a prosthesis. This will make the level of the award towards the top end of the bracket.

Amputation through the elbow will normally produce an award at the bottom end of the bracket.

		with 10% uplift
(iii) Below-elbow Amputation	£70,650 to £80,600	£77,715 to £88,660

Amputation through the forearm with residual severe organic and phantom pains would attract an award at the top end of the bracket.

(F) OTHER ARM INJURIES

(a) Severe Injuries	£70,650 to £96,250	£77,715 to £105,875

Injuries which fall short of amputation but which are extremely serious and leave the injured person little better off than if the arm had been lost; for example, a serious brachial plexus injury.

(b) Injuries resulting in Permanent and Substantial Disablement	£28,750 to £44,000	£31,625 to £48,400

Serious fractures of one or both forearms where there is significant permanent residual disability whether functional or cosmetic.

(c) Less Severe Injury	£14,100 to £28,750	£15,510 to £31,625

While there will have been significant disabilities, a substantial degree of recovery will have taken place or will be expected.

		with 10% uplift
(d) Simple Fractures of the Forearm	**£4,900 to £14,100**	£5,390 to £15,510

(G) Injuries to the Elbow

(a) A Severely Disabling Injury	**£28,750 to £40,300**	£31,625 to £44,330
(b) Less Severe Injuries	**£11,500 to £23,500**	£12,650 to £25,850

Injuries causing impairment of function but not involving major surgery or significant disability.

(c) Moderate or Minor Injury	up to **£9,250**	up to £10,175

Most elbow injuries fall into this category. They comprise simple fractures, tennis elbow syndrome and lacerations; i.e., those injuries which cause no permanent damage and do not result in any permanent impairment of function.

(i) Injuries fully resolving after about one year will usually attract an award in the region of £2,600 (£2,860 accounting for 10% uplift)

(ii) Injuries with the majority of symptoms resolving within 18 to 24 months but with nuisance level symptoms persisting after that would attract an award of £4,600 (£5,060 accounting for 10% uplift)

(iii) Injuries recovering after three years with nuisance symptoms thereafter and/or requiring surgery will attract awards towards the top of the bracket.

(H) WRIST INJURIES

with 10% uplift

(a)	Injuries resulting in complete loss of function in the wrist, for example, where an arthrodesis has been performed.	**£35,000 to £44,000**	£38,500 to £48,400
(b)	Injury resulting in significant permanent disability, but where some useful movement remains.	**£18,000 to £28,750**	£19,800 to £31,625
(c)	Less severe injuries where these still result in some permanent disability as, for example, a degree of persisting pain and stiffness.	**£9,250 to £18,000**	£10,175 to £19,800
(d)	Where recovery from fracture or soft tissue injury takes longer but is complete, the award will rarely exceed £7,500 (£8,250 with 10% uplift).		
(e)	An uncomplicated Colles' fracture.	**In the region of £5,450**	In the region of £5,995
(f)	Very minor undisplaced or minimally displaced fractures and soft tissue injuries necessitating application of plaster or bandage for a matter of weeks and a full or virtual recovery within up to 12 months or so.	**£2,600 to £3,500**	£2,860 to £3,850

(I) HAND INJURIES

The hands are cosmetically and functionally the most important component parts of the upper limbs. The loss of a hand is valued not far short of the amount which would be awarded for the loss of the arm itself. The upper end of any bracket will generally be appropriate where the injury is to the dominant hand.

In cases of injuries to multiple digits, practitioners and Judges should not simply add the figures which would be appropriate for each injury separately, but should consider the overall extent of pain, suffering and loss of amenity, usually leading to a lower award than would be appropriate by simple addition.

			with 10% uplift
(a)	**Total or Effective Loss of Both Hands**	**£103,250 to £148,000**	£113,575 to £162,800

Serious injury resulting in extensive damage to both hands such as to render them little more than useless. The top of the bracket is applicable where no effective prosthesis can be used.

(b)	**Serious Damage to Both Hands**	**£41,300 to £62,150**	£45,430 to £68,365

Such injuries will have given rise to permanent cosmetic disability and significant loss of function.

(c)	**Total or Effective Loss of One Hand**	**£70,650 to £80,600**	£77,715 to £88,660

This bracket will apply to a hand which was crushed and thereafter surgically amputated or where all fingers and most of the palm have been traumatically amputated. The upper end of the bracket is indicated where the hand so damaged was the dominant one.

			with 10% uplift
(d)	**Amputation of Index and Middle and/or Ring Fingers**	**£45,500 to £66,650**	£50,050 to £73,315

The hand will have been rendered of very little use and such grip as remains will be exceedingly weak.

(e)	**Serious Hand Injuries**	**£21,300 to £45,500**	£23,430 to £50,050

Such injuries will, for example, have reduced the hand to about 50 per cent capacity. Included would be cases where several fingers have been amputated but rejoined to the hand leaving it clawed, clumsy and unsightly, or amputation of some fingers together with part of the palm resulting in gross diminution of grip and dexterity and gross cosmetic disfigurement.

(f)	**Less Serious Hand Injury**	**£10,600 to £21,300**	£11,660 to £23,430

Such as a severe crush injury resulting in significantly impaired function without future surgery or despite operative treatment undergone.

(g)	**Moderate Hand Injury**	**£4,600 to £9,750**	£5,060 to £10,725

Crush injuries, penetrating wounds, soft tissue type and deep lacerations. The top of the bracket would be appropriate where surgery has failed and permanent disability remains.

			with 10% uplift
(h)	**Minor Hand Injuries**	**£670 to £3,190**	£737 to £3,509

Injuries similar to but less serious than (g) above with recovery within a few months.

(i)	**Severe Fractures to Fingers**	**up to £27,000**	up to £29,700

These may lead to partial amputations and result in deformity, impairment of grip, reduced mechanical function and disturbed sensation.

(j)	**Total Loss of Index Finger**	**In the region of £13,750**	In the region of £15,125

(k)	**Partial Loss of Index Finger**	**£8,950 to £13,750**	£9,845 to £15,125

This bracket also covers cases of injury to the index finger giving rise to disfigurement and impairment of grip or dexterity.

(l)	**Fracture of Index Finger**	**£6,700 to £9,000**	£7,370 to £9,900

This level is appropriate where a fracture has mended quickly but grip has remained impaired, there is pain on heavy use and osteoarthritis is likely in due course.

(m)	**Total Loss of Middle Finger**	**In the region of £11,500**	In the region of £12,650

(n)	**Serious Injury to Ring or Middle Fingers**	**£11,000 to £12,000**	£12,100 to £13,200

Fractures or serious injury to tendons causing stiffness, deformity and permanent loss of grip or dexterity will fall within this bracket.

			with 10% uplift
(o)	**Loss of the Terminal Phalanx of the Ring or Middle Fingers**	**£2,900 to £5,750**	£3,190 to £6,325
(p)	**Amputation of Little Finger**	**£6,350 to £9,000**	£6,985 to £9,900
(q)	**Loss of Part of the Little Finger**	**£2,900 to £4,300**	£3,190 to £4,730

(q) This is appropriate where the remaining tip is sensitive.

(r)	**Amputation of Ring and Little Fingers**	**In the region of £16,000**	In the region of £17,600
(s)	**Amputation of the Terminal Phalanges of the Index and Middle Fingers**	**In the region of £18,350**	In the region of £20,185

(s) Such injury will involve scarring, restriction of movement and impairment of grip and fine handling.

(t)	**Fracture of One Finger**	**up to £3,500**	up to £3,850

(t) Depending upon recovery time.

(u)	**Loss of Thumb**	**£26,100 to £40,300**	£28,710 to £44,330
(v)	**Very Serious Injury to Thumb**	**£14,400 to £25,750**	£15,840 to £28,325

(v) This bracket is appropriate where the thumb has been severed at the base and grafted back leaving a virtually useless and deformed digit, or where the thumb has been amputated through the interphalangeal joint.

			with 10% uplift
(w)	**Serious Injury to the Thumb**	£9,250 to £12,300	£10,175 to £13,530

Such injuries may involve amputation of the tip, nerve damage or fracture necessitating the insertion of wires as a result of which the thumb is cold and ultra-sensitive and there is impaired grip and loss of manual dexterity.

(x)	**Moderate Injuries to the Thumb**	£7,100 to £9,250	£7,810 to £10,175

These are injuries such as those necessitating arthrodesis of the interphalangeal joint or causing damage to tendons or nerves. Such injuries result in impairment of sensation and function and cosmetic deformity.

(y)	**Severe Dislocation of the Thumb**	£2,900 to £5,000	£3,190 to £5,500
(z)	**Minor Injuries to the Thumb**	up to £2,900	up to £3,190

Such an injury would be a fracture which has recovered in six months except for residual stiffness and some discomfort.

(aa)	**Trivial Thumb Injuries**	up to £1,620	up to £1,782

These may have caused severe pain for a very short time but will have resolved within a few months.

(J) VIBRATION WHITE FINGER (VWF) AND/OR HAND ARM VIBRATION SYNDROME (HAVS)

Vibration White Finger and/or Hand Arm Vibration Syndrome, caused by exposure to vibration, is a slowly progressive condition, the development and severity of which are affected by the degree of exposure, in particular the magnitude, frequency, duration and transmission of the vibration. The symptoms are similar to those experienced in the constitutional condition of Raynaud's phenomenon.

The Stockholm Workshop Scale is now the accepted table for medical grading of the severity of the condition. The Scale classifies both the vascular and sensorineural components in two complementary tables. Individual assessment is made separately for each hand and for each finger.

The vascular component is graded between Stage 0V (no attacks) through mild, moderate and severe to 4V (very severe) where there are frequent attacks affecting all phalanges of most fingers with atrophic changes in the fingertips. The sensorineural component is graded between Stage 0SN (no symptoms) and 3SN (intermittent or persistent numbness, reduced tactile discrimination and/or manipulative dexterity). The grade of disorder is indicated by the stage and number of affected fingers on both hands.

Any interference with work or social life is disregarded in that grading.

The assessment of damages is therefore not strictly tied to the Stockholm Workshop

Scale grading. It depends more on the extent of the symptoms and their impact, having regard to the following factors:

(i) age at onset;

(ii) whether one or both hands are affected and, if only one, whether it is the dominant hand;

(iii) number of fingers affected;

(iv) extent of impaired dexterity and/or reduction in grip strength;

(v) frequency and duration of painful episodes;

(vi) effect of symptoms on work, domestic and social life.

Accordingly, depending on individual circumstances, a lower award might be made despite significant Stockholm Workshop Scale grading where, e.g., employment is unaffected, whilst a higher award might be attracted where there is a lesser grading but a greater impact on normal life.

In a severe case, the injury may be regarded as damaging a hand rather than being confined to the fingers.

The brackets can best be defined and valued as follows (note that it is not intended that these should correlate directly with the Stockholm Workshop Scale):

			with 10% uplift
(a)	**Most Serious**	£23,250 to £28,250	£25,575 to £31,075

Persisting bilateral symptoms in a younger person which interfere significantly with daily life and lead to a change in employment.

		with 10% uplift
(b) **Serious**	**£12,300** **to £23,250**	£13,530 to £25,575

In this bracket there will have been a marked interference with work and domestic activity. Attacks may occur throughout the year.

(c) **Moderate**	**£6,350** **to £12,300**	£6,985 to £13,530

This bracket will include claimants in their middle years where employment has been maintained or varied only to remove excess vibration. Attacks will occur mostly in cold weather.

(d) **Minor**	**£2,200** **to £6,350**	£2,420 to £6,985

Occasional symptoms in only a few fingers with a modest effect on work or leisure.

(K) WORK-RELATED UPPER LIMB DISORDERS

This section covers a range of upper limb injury in the form of the following pathological conditions:

(a) Tenosynovitis: inflammation of synovial sheaths of tendons usually resolving with rest over a short period. Sometimes this condition leads to continuing symptoms of loss of grip and dexterity.

(b) De Quervain's tenosynovitis: a form of tenosynovitis, rarely bilateral, involving inflammation of the tendons of the thumb.

(c) Stenosing tenosynovitis: otherwise, trigger finger/thumb: thickening tendons.

(d) Carpal tunnel syndrome: constriction of the median nerve of the wrist or thickening of surrounding tissue. It is often relieved by a decompression operation.

(e) Epicondylitis: inflammation in the elbow joint: medial = golfer's elbow; lateral = tennis elbow. The brackets below apply to all these conditions but the level of the award is affected by the following considerations regardless of the precise condition:

   (i) are the effects bilateral or one sided (and, if one-sided, whether it is the dominant hand)?

   (ii) the level of symptoms, i.e., pain, swelling, tenderness, crepitus;

   (iii) the ability to work and the effect on domestic and social life;

   (iv) the capacity to avoid the recurrence of symptoms;

   (v) surgery;

   (vi) age;

   (vii) which, if any, of the symptoms would have been suffered in any event and when.

			with 10% uplift
(a)	Continuing bilateral disability with surgery and loss of employment.	**£16,100 to £17,000**	£17,710 to £18,700
(b)	Continuing, but fluctuating and unilateral symptoms.	**£11,000 to £12,000**	£12,100 to £13,200
(c)	Symptoms resolving in the course of up to three years.	**£6,350 to £7,900**	£6,985 to £8,690
(d)	Complete recovery within a short period (of weeks or a few months)	**£1,620 to £2,600**	£1,782 to £2,860

(L) Leg Injuries

(a) Amputations

(i) Loss of Both Legs   **£177,000 to £207,250**   £194,700 to £227,975

This is the appropriate award where both legs are lost above the knee or one leg has been lost above the knee at a high level and the other leg has been lost below the knee. The level of award will be determined by factors such as the severity of any phantom pains; associated psychological problems; the success of any prosthetics; any side effects such as backache and the risk of future degenerative changes in the hips and spine.

(ii) Below-knee Amputation of Both Legs   **£148,000 to £198,500**   £162,800 to £218,350

The level of the amputations will be important, with an award at the top of the bracket appropriate where both legs are amputated just below the knee. Otherwise, the award will depend upon factors such as the severity of any phantom pains; associated psychological problems; the success of any prosthetics; any side effects such as backache and the risk of developing degenerative changes in the remaining joints of both lower limbs or in the hips and spine.

		with 10% uplift
(iii) Above-knee Amputation of One Leg	**£77,000 to £101,000**	£84,700 to £111,100

The award will depend upon such factors as the level of the amputation; the severity of any phantom pains; associated psychological problems; the success of any prosthetics; any side effects such as backache and the risk of developing osteoarthritis in the remaining joints of both lower limbs or in the hips and spine.

(iv) Below-knee Amputation of One Leg	**£72,000 to £97,750**	£79,200 to £107,525

The straightforward case of a below-knee amputation with no complications would justify an award towards the bottom of this bracket. At or towards the top of the range would come the traumatic amputation which occurs in a devastating accident, where the injured person remained fully conscious, or cases where attempts to save the leg led to numerous unsuccessful operations so that amputation occurred years after the event. Factors such as phantom pains, the success of any prosthetics, associated psychological problems and the increased chance of developing osteoarthritis in the remaining joints of both limbs will also be important in determining the appropriate award.

(b) Severe Leg Injuries

with 10% uplift

(i) The Most Serious Injuries Short of Amputation

£70,750 to £100,000   £77,825 to £110,000

Some injuries, although not involving amputation, are so severe that the courts have awarded damages at a similar level. Such injuries would include extensive degloving of the leg, where there is gross shortening of the leg or where fractures have not united and extensive bone grafting has been undertaken.

(ii) Very Serious

£40,300 to £62,150   £44,330 to £68,365

Injuries leading to permanent problems with mobility, the need for crutches or mobility aids for the remainder of the injured person's life; injuries where multiple fractures have taken years to heal, required extensive treatment and have led to serious deformity and limitation of movement, or where arthritis has developed in a joint so that further surgical treatment is likely.

(iii) Serious

£28,800 to £40,300   £31,680 to £44,330

Serious compound or comminuted fractures or injuries to joints or ligaments resulting in instability, prolonged treatment, a lengthy period of non-weight-bearing, the near certainty that arthritis will ensue; extensive scarring. To justify an award within this bracket a combination of such features will generally be necessary.

		with 10% uplift
(iv) Moderate	**£20,400 to £28,800**	£22,440 to £31,680

This bracket includes complicated or multiple fractures or severe crushing injuries, generally to a single limb. The level of an award within the bracket will be influenced by the extent of treatment undertaken; impact on employment; the presence or risk of degenerative changes and/or future surgery; imperfect union of fractures, muscle wasting; limited joint movements; instability in the knee; unsightly scarring or permanently increased vulnerability to future damage.

(c) Less Serious Leg Injuries

(i) Fractures from which an Incomplete Recovery is Made or Serious Soft Tissue Injuries	**£13,200 to £20,400**	£14,520 to £22,440

In the case of fracture injuries, the injured person will have made a reasonable recovery but will be left with a metal implant and/or defective gait, a limp, impaired mobility, sensory loss, discomfort or an exacerbation of a pre-existing disability. This bracket will also involve serious soft tissue injuries to one or both legs causing significant cosmetic deficit, functional restriction and/or some nerve damage in the lower limbs.

			with 10% uplift
(ii)	Simple Fracture of a Femur with No Damage to Articular Surfaces	**£6,700 to £10,350**	£7,370 to £11,385
(iii)	Simple Fractures and Soft Tissue Injuries	**up to £6,700**	up to £7,370

Towards the top of the bracket will come simple fractures of the tibia or fibula from which a complete recovery has been made. The level of award will be influenced by time spent in plaster and the length of the recovery period. Below this level fall a wide variety of soft tissue injuries, lacerations, cuts, bruising or contusions, all of which have recovered completely or almost so and any residual disability is cosmetic or of a minor nature. Where these modest injuries have fully resolved within a few months an award of less than £1,800 (£1,980 accounting for 10% uplift) is likely to be justified.

(M) Knee Injuries

(a) Severe

(i)	Serious knee injury where there has been disruption of the joint,	**£51,250 to £70,700**	£56,375 to £77,770

the development of osteoarthritis, gross ligamentous damage, lengthy treatment, considerable pain and loss of function and an arthroplasty or arthrodesis has taken place or is inevitable.

		with 10% uplift
(ii) Leg fracture extending into the knee joint causing pain which is constant, permanent, limiting movement or impairing agility and rendering the injured person prone to osteoarthritis and at risk of arthroplasty.	**£38,300 to £51,250**	£42,130 to £56,375
(iii) Less severe injuries than those in (a)(ii) above and/or injuries which result in less severe disability. There may be continuing symptoms by way of pain and discomfort and limitation of movement or instability or deformity with the risk that degenerative changes and the need for remedial surgery may occur in the long term as a result of damage to the kneecap, ligamentous or meniscal injury or muscular wasting.	**£19,250 to £32,000**	£21,175 to £35,200

(b) Moderate

(i) Injuries involving dislocation, torn cartilage or meniscus which results in minor instability, wasting, weakness or other mild future disability. This bracket also includes injuries which accelerate symptoms from a pre-existing condition over a prolonged period of years.	**£10,900 to £19,250**	£11,990 to £21,175

with 10% uplift

(ii) This bracket includes injuries similar to those in (b)(i) above, but less serious and involving shorter periods of acceleration, and also lacerations, twisting or bruising injuries. Where there is continuous aching or discomfort, or occasional pain, the award will be towards the upper end of the bracket. Where recovery has been complete the award is unlikely to exceed £4,300 (£4,730 accounting for 10% uplift). Modest injuries that resolve within a short space of time will attract lower awards.	**up to £10,100**	up to £11,110

(N) ANKLE INJURIES

(a) **Very Severe** Examples of injuries falling within this bracket are limited and unusual. They include cases of a transmalleolar fracture of the ankle with extensive soft-tissue damage resulting in deformity and the risk that any future injury to the leg might necessitate a below-knee amputation, or cases of bilateral ankle fractures causing degeneration of the joints at a young age so that arthrodesis is necessary.	**£36,800 to £51,200**	£40,480 to £56,320
(b) **Severe** Injuries necessitating an extensive period of treatment and/or a lengthy period in plaster or where pins and plates have been inserted and there is significant residual	**£23,000 to £36,800**	£25,300 to £40,480

disability in the form of ankle instability and severely limited ability to walk. The level of the award within the bracket will be determined in part by such features as a failed arthrodesis, the presence of or risk of osteoarthritis, regular sleep disturbance, unsightly scarring, impact on employment and any need to wear special footwear.

		with 10% uplift
(c) Moderate	**£10,100 to £19,550**	**£11,110 to £21,505**

Fractures, ligamentous tears and the like which give rise to less serious disabilities such as difficulty in walking on uneven ground, difficulty standing or walking for long periods of time, awkwardness on stairs, irritation from metal plates and residual scarring There may also be a risk of future osteoarthritis.

(d) Modest Injuries	**up to £10,100**	**up to £11,110**

The less serious, minor or undisplaced fractures, sprains and ligamentous injuries. The level of the award within the bracket will be determined by whether or not a complete recovery has been made and, if recovery is incomplete, whether there is any tendency for the ankle to give way, and whether there is scarring, aching or discomfort, loss of movement or the possibility of long-term osteoarthritis.

Where recovery is complete without any ongoing symptoms or scarring, the award is unlikely to exceed £5,650 (£6,215 accounting for 10% uplift). Where recovery is complete within a year, the award is unlikely to exceed £4,050 (£4,455 accounting for 10% uplift). Modest

injuries that resolve within a short space
of time will attract lower awards.

(O) ACHILLES TENDON

		with 10% uplift
(a) Most Serious	**In the region of £28,250**	In the region of £31,075

Severance of the tendon and the peroneus
longus muscle giving rise to cramp,
swelling and restricted ankle movement
necessitating the cessation of active
sports.

(b) Serious	**£18,350 to £22,100**	£20,185 to £24,310

Where complete division of the tendon
has been successfully repaired but there
is residual weakness, a limitation of
ankle movements, a limp and residual
scarring and where further improvement
is unlikely.

(c) Moderate	**£9,250 to £15,500**	£10,175 to £17,050

Cases involving partial rupture or
significant injury to the tendon. The
level of award within the bracket will be
determined by the treatment received
(whether conservative or invasive), the
level of recovery made, ongoing pain,
any continuing functional disability and
permanent scarring.

		with 10% uplift
(d) **Minor**	**£5,350** **to £9,250**	£5,885 to £10,175

A turning of the ankle resulting in some damage to the tendon and a feeling of being unsure of ankle support would fall within this bracket. The consequences of these injuries may be similar to modest ankle injuries and further guidance may be obtained from bracket (N)(d).

(P) FOOT INJURIES

(a) **Amputation of Both Feet**	**£124,500** **to £148,000**	£136,950 to £162,800

This injury is treated similarly to below-knee amputation of both legs because the common feature is loss of a useful ankle joint.

(b) **Amputation of One Foot**	**£61,700** **to £80,600**	£67,870 to £88,660

This injury is also treated as similar to a below-knee amputation because of the loss of the ankle joint.

(c) **Very Severe**	**£61,700** **to £80,600**	£67,870 to £88,660

To fall within this bracket the injury must produce permanent and severe pain or really serious permanent disability. Examples would include the traumatic amputation of the forefoot where there was a significant risk of the need for a full amputation and serious exacerbation of an existing back problem, or cases of the

loss of a substantial portion of the heel so
that mobility was grossly restricted.

			with 10% uplift
(d)	**Severe**	**£30,850 to £51,500**	£33,935 to £56,650

Fractures of *both* heels or feet with a
substantial restriction on mobility or
considerable and permanent pain. The
bracket will also include unusually
severe injury to a single foot. Examples
include injuries that result in severe
degloving, extensive surgery, heel fusion,
osteoporosis, ulceration or other disability
preventing the wearing of ordinary shoes.
It will also apply in the case of a drop foot
deformity corrected by a brace.

(e)	**Serious**	**£18,350 to £28,800**	£20,185 to £31,680

This bracket will include injuries less
severe than in (d) above but leading to
continuing pain from traumatic arthritis
or the risk of future arthritis, prolonged
treatment and the risk of fusion surgery.

(f)	**Moderate**	**£10,100 to £18,350**	£11,110 to £20,185

Displaced metatarsal fractures resulting
in permanent deformity and continuing
symptoms. There may be a risk of long-
term osteoarthritis and/or future surgery.

(g)	**Modest**	**up to £10,100**	up to £11,110

Simple metatarsal fractures, ruptured
ligaments, puncture wounds and the like.
Where there are continuing symptoms,

such as a permanent limp, pain or aching, awards between £5,150 (£5,665 accounting for 10% uplift) and £10,100 (£11,110 accounting for 10% uplift) would be appropriate. Straightforward foot injuries such as fractures, lacerations, contusions etc. from which complete or near complete recovery is made would justify awards of £5,150 (£5,665 accounting for 10% uplift) or less. Modest injuries that resolve within a short space of time will attract lower awards.

(Q) TOE INJURIES

			with 10% uplift
(a)	**Amputation of All Toes**	**£26,850 to £41,250**	£29,535 to £45,375

The position within the bracket will be determined by, for example, whether or not the amputation was traumatic or surgical and the extent of the loss of the forefoot together with the residual effects on mobility.

(b)	**Amputation of the Great Toe**	**In the region of £23,000**	In the region of £25,300

(c)	**Severe Toe Injuries**	**£10,100 to £15,500**	£11,110 to £17,050

This is the appropriate bracket for severe crush injuries, leading to amputation of one or two toes (other than the great toe) or falling short of the need for amputation or necessitating only partial amputation. It also includes bursting wounds and injuries resulting in severe damage and in any event producing significant continuing symptoms.

		with 10% uplift
(d) **Serious Toe Injuries**	**£7,050 to £10,100**	£7,755 to £11,110

Such injuries will be serious injuries to the great toe or crush and multiple fractures of two or more toes. There will be some permanent disability by way of discomfort, pain or sensitive scarring to justify an award within this bracket. Where there have been a number of unsuccessful operations or persisting stabbing pains, impaired gait or the like the award will tend towards the top end of the bracket.

(e) **Moderate Toe Injuries**	**up to £7,050**	up to £7,755

These injuries include relatively straight-forward fractures or the exacerbation of a pre-existing degenerative condition. Cases involving prolonged minor symptoms are likely to justify awards towards the upper end of this bracket. Only £4,110 (£4,521 accounting for 10% uplift) or less would be awarded for straightforward fractures or crushing/soft tissue injuries of one or more toes with complete resolution or near complete resolution. Modest injuries that resolve within a short space of time will attract lower awards.

8

Chronic Pain

This chapter deals with a variety of what may loosely be described as 'pain disorders'. This includes Fibromyalgia, Chronic Pain Syndrome, Chronic Fatigue Syndrome (also known as ME), Conversion Disorders (also known as Dissociative Disorders) and Somatoform Disorders. Many such disorders are characterized by subjective pain without any, or any commensurate, organic basis. The figures given here assume causation of relevant symptoms is established. Cases of short-lived pain disorders, short-term exacerbation of an existing pain disorder, or brief acceleration of the onset of a pain disorder, all fall outside the suggested brackets and will require separate consideration.

With the exception of cases of Complex Regional Pain Syndrome, no attempt has been made to sub-divide between different clinical conditions. Guidance instead reflects the impact, severity, and prognosis of the condition. Where the condition principally affects a single part of the anatomy, cross-reference to the relevant chapter within the Judicial College Guidelines may assist.

The factors to be taken into account in valuing claims for pain disorders (including CRPS) include the following:

(i) the degree of pain experienced;

(ii) the overall impact of the symptoms (which may include fatigue, associated impairments of cognitive function, muscle weakness, headaches etc. and taking account of any fluctuation in symptoms) on mobility, ability to function in daily life and the need for care/assistance;

(iii) the effect of the condition on the injured person's ability to work;

(iv) the need to take medication to control symptoms of pain and the effect of such medication on the person's ability to function in normal daily life;

(v) the extent to which treatment has been undertaken and its effect (or its predicted effect in respect of future treatment);

(vi) whether the condition is limited to one anatomical site or is widespread;

(vii) the presence of any separately identifiable psychiatric disorder and its impact on the perception of pain;

(viii) the age of the claimant;

(ix) prognosis.

(a) **Complex Regional Pain Syndrome ('CRPS')—also known as Reflex Sympathetic Dystrophy**

The condition is characterized by intense, burning pain which can make moving or even touching the affected limb intolerable.

			with 10% uplift
(i)	Severe: in such cases the prognosis will be poor; ability to work will be greatly reduced if not completely eliminated; significant care/domestic assistance needs; co-existing psychological problems may be present. At the top end of the scale, symptoms may have spread to other limbs.	**£38,600 to £61,750**	£42,460 to £67,925
(ii)	Moderate: the top end of this bracket will include cases where significant effects have been experienced for a prolonged period but prognosis assumes some future improvement enabling a return to work in a significant (not necessarily full-time) capacity and with only modest future care requirements. At the lower end will be cases where symptoms have persisted for some years but are more variable in intensity, where medication is effective in limiting symptoms and/or where the prognosis is markedly better, though not necessarily for complete resolution. May already have resumed employment. Minimal, if any, future care requirements.	**£20,600 to £38,600**	£22,660 to £42,460

(b) Other Pain Disorders

(i)	Severe: In these cases significant symptoms will be on-going despite treatment and will be expected to persist, resulting in adverse impact on ability to work and the need for some care/assistance. Most cases of	**£31,000 to £46,300**	£34,100 to £50,930

Fibromyalgia with serious persisting
symptoms will fall within the range.

(ii) Moderate: At the top end of this **£15,500** £17,050
bracket are cases where symptoms **to £28,300** to £31,130
are on-going, albeit of lesser degree
than in (i) above and the impact on
ability to work/function in daily life
is less marked. At the bottom end
are cases where full, or near complete recovery has been made (or is
anticipated) after symptoms have
persisted for a number of years.

9

Facial Injuries

The assessment of general damages for facial injuries is an extremely difficult task, there being three elements which complicate the award.

First, while in most of the cases dealt with below the injuries described are skeletal, many of them will involve an element of disfigurement or at least some cosmetic effect.

Second, in cases where there is a cosmetic element the courts have hitherto drawn a distinction between the awards of damages to males and females, the latter attracting the higher awards. That distinction, arising from cases that stretch back into the mists of time, has been reflected in succeeding editions of these Guidelines. It is nonetheless open to serious doubt that gender itself can be a proper or indeed lawful factor in determining the level of general damages. That is not to say that factors which inform the appropriate level of general damages for scarring may not arise more commonly, or with more general potency, in the case of one gender rather than another. Older cases in particular may need to be viewed with a degree of caution. The Guideline has retained the 'female' and 'male' sections because that is the historical approach. We await a judicial decision synthesising the two.

Third, in cases of disfigurement there may also be severe psychological reactions which put the total award at the top of the bracket, or above it altogether.

(A) SKELETAL INJURIES

		with 10% uplift
(a) Le Fort Fractures of Frontal Facial Bones	**£17,500 to £27,000**	£19,250 to £29,700
(b) Multiple Fractures of Facial Bones	**£11,000 to £17,600**	£12,100 to £19,360

(b) Multiple Fractures of Facial Bones

Involving some facial deformity of a permanent nature.

(c) Fractures of Nose or Nasal Complex

(i) Serious or multiple fractures requiring a number of operations and/or resulting in permanent damage to airways and/or nerves or tear ducts and/or facial deformity.	**£7,800 to £17,000**	£8,580 to £18,700
(ii) Displaced fracture where recovery complete but only after surgery.	**£2,900 to £3,750**	£3,190 to £4,125
(iii) Displaced fracture requiring no more than manipulation.	**£1,850 to £2,300**	£2,035 to £2,530
(iv) Simple undisplaced fracture with full recovery.	**£1,250 to £1,850**	£1,375 to £2,035

(d) Fractures of Cheekbones

with 10% uplift

(i) Serious fractures requiring surgery but with lasting consequences such as paraesthesia in the cheeks or the lips or some element of disfigurement.	**£7,500 to £11,600**	£8,250 to £12,760
(ii) Simple fracture of cheekbones for which some reconstructive surgery is necessary but from which there is a complete recovery with no or only minimal cosmetic effects.	**£3,200 to £4,750**	£3,520 to £5,225
(iii) Simple fracture of cheekbone for which no surgery is required and where a complete recovery is effected.	**£1,700 to £2,200**	£1,870 to £2,420

(e) Fractures of Jaws

(i) Very serious multiple fractures followed by prolonged treatment and permanent consequences, including severe pain, restriction in eating, paraesthesia and/or the risk of arthritis in the joints.	**£22,400 to £33,500**	£24,640 to £36,850
(ii) Serious fracture with permanent consequences such as difficulty in opening the mouth or with eating or where there is paraesthesia in the area of the jaw.	**£13,200 to £22,400**	£14,520 to £24,640
(iii) Simple fracture requiring immobilisation but from which recovery is complete.	**£4,750 to £6,400**	£5,225 to £7,040

(f) Damage to Teeth

In these cases there will generally have been a course of treatment as a result of the initial injury. The amounts awarded will vary according to the extent and/or the degree of discomfort of such treatment. Any difficulty with eating increases the award. These cases may overlap with fractures of the jaw, meriting awards in the brackets for such fractures. Awards may be greater where the damage results in or is caused by protracted dentistry.

		with 10% uplift
Significant, chronic, tooth pain (such as from an untreated abscess) extending over a number of years together with significant general deterioration in the overall condition of teeth:	up to £28,000	up to £30,800
(i) Loss of or serious damage to several front teeth.	£6,400 to £8,400	£7,040 to £9,240
(ii) Loss of or serious damage to two front teeth.	£3,200 to £5,600	£3,520 to £6,160
(iii) Loss of or serious damage to one front tooth.	£1,620 to £2,900	£1,782 to £3,190
(iv) Loss of or damage to back teeth: per tooth:	£800 to £1,250	£880 to £1,375

(B) FACIAL DISFIGUREMENT

In this class of case a number of common factors fall to be considered:

- the nature of the underlying injury which has resulted in facial disfigurement;

- the nature and extent of treatment;

- the nature and extent of the residual scarring or disfigurement;

- the age of the claimant;

- the subjective impact on the disfigurement upon the claimant and the extent to which it adversely affects the claimant's social, domestic and work lives;

- the psychological impact upon the claimant, which in severe cases may be very substantial.

The subject of burns is not dealt with separately. Burns of any degree of severity are particularly painful and disfiguring, and awards are invariably at the upper ends of the brackets, or above them altogether. The very worst burns may lead not only to considerable disfigurement and pain but to a variety of continuing physical and psychological injuries meriting very high awards. See also the general guidance in relation to burn injuries in Chapter 10.

As explained earlier, it is doubtful that gender alone can justify different levels of award. The two sets of figures may be regarded as overlapping.

(a) Females

		with 10% uplift
(i) Very Severe Scarring	£35,600 to £71,500	£39,160 to £78,650

In relatively young women (typically teens to early 30s), where the cosmetic effect is very disfiguring and the psychological reaction severe.

		with 10% uplift
(ii) Less Severe Scarring	**£22,300 to £35,600**	£24,530 to £39,160

Where the disfigurement is still substantial and where there is a significant psychological reaction.

(iii) Significant Scarring	**£13,200 to £22,100**	£14,520 to £24,310

Where the worst effects have been or will be reduced by plastic surgery leaving some cosmetic disability and where the psychological reaction is not great or, having been considerable at the outset, has diminished to relatively minor proportions.

(iv) Less Significant Scarring	**£2,900 to £10,100**	£3,190 to £11,110

In these cases there may be but one scar which can be camouflaged or, though there is a number of very small scars, the overall effect is to mar but not markedly to affect the appearance and the reaction is no more than that of an ordinarily sensitive young woman.

(v) Trivial Scarring	**£1,250 to £2,600**	£1,375 to £2,860

In these cases the effect is minor only.

(b) Males

(i) Very Severe Scarring	**£21,900 to £48,250**	£24,090 to £53,075

These are to be found especially in males under 30, where there is permanent disfigurement even after plastic surgery and a considerable element of psychological reaction.

			with 10% uplift
(ii)	Less Severe Scarring	**£13,200 to £22,100**	£14,520 to £24,310
	This will have left moderate to severe permanent disfigurement.		
(iii)	Significant Scarring	**£6,700 to £13,200**	£7,370 to £14,520
	Such scars will remain visible at conversational distances.		
(iv)	Less Significant Scarring	**£2,900 to £6,700**	£3,190 to £7,370
	Such scarring is not particularly prominent except on close inspection.		
(v)	Trivial Scarring	**£1,250 to £2,600**	£1,375 to £2,860
	In these cases the effect is minor only.		

10

Scarring to Other Parts of the Body

This is an area in which it is not possible to offer much useful guidance. The principles (including the approach to awards for different genders) are the same as those applied to cases of facial disfigurement. It must be remembered that many of the physical injuries already described involve some element of disfigurement and that element is of course taken into account in suggesting the appropriate bracket. There remain some cases where the element of disfigurement is the predominant one in the assessment of damages. Where the scarring is not to the face or is not usually visible then the awards will tend to be lower than those for facial or readily visible disfigurement.

		with 10% uplift
A large proportion of awards for a number of noticeable laceration scars, or a single disfiguring scar, of leg(s) or arm(s) or hand(s) or back or chest (male), fall in the bracket of £5,500 to £16,700.	**£5,500 to £16,700**	£6,050 to £18,370
In cases where an exploratory laparotomy has been performed but no significant internal injury has been found, the award for the operation and the inevitable scar is in the region of £6,350.	**In the region of £6,350**	In the region of £6,985

		with 10% uplift
A single noticeable scar, or several superficial scars, of leg(s) or arm(s) or hand(s), with some minor cosmetic deficit justifies £1,750 to £5,600.	**£1,750 to £5,600**	£1,925 to £6,160
As we have noted in Chapter 9, the effects of burns will normally be regarded as more serious since they tend to cause a greater degree of pain and may lead to continuing physical and psychological injury. Serious burn injuries will attract very significant awards. Where significant burns cover 40% or more of the body, awards are likely to exceed £77,000. Factors which will influence the size of award in burns cases will include:	**Likely to exceed £77,000**	Likely to exceed £84,700

(a) The percentage body area affected by the burns;

(b) Whether the burns are full thickness, partial thickness or superficial;

(c) The cosmetic impact of the injuries and the injured person's reactions to them;

(d) The need for (and extent of) surgery;

(e) Any resulting physical disability;

(f) The psychological impact.

11

Damage to Hair

			with 10% uplift
(a)	Damage to hair in consequence of defective permanent waving, tinting or the like, where the effects are dermatitis or tingling or 'burning' of the scalp causing dry, brittle hair, which breaks off and/or falls out, leading to distress, depression, embarrassment and loss of confidence, and inhibiting social life. In the more serious cases thinning continues and the prospects of regrowth are poor or there has been total loss of areas of hair and regrowth is slow.	**£5,400 to £8,100**	£5,940 to £8,910
	There may be a larger award in cases of significant psychological disability or if surgical intervention (e.g. skin grafting) is required.		
(b)	Less serious versions of the above where symptoms are fewer or only of a minor character; also, cases where hair has been pulled out leaving bald patches. The level of the award will depend on the length of time taken before regrowth occurs.	**£2,900 to £5,400**	£3,190 to £5,940

12

Dermatitis

Apart from dermatitis of the scalp (see Chapter 11), most of the reported cases relate to dermatitis of the hands. Higher awards are likely to be justified where the face is affected.

			with 10% uplift
(a)	Dermatitis of both hands, with cracking and soreness, affecting employment and domestic capability, possibly with some psychological consequences, lasting for some years, perhaps indefinitely.	**£10,100 to £14,100**	£11,110 to £15,510
(b)	Dermatitis of one or both hands, continuing for a significant period, but settling with treatment and/or use of gloves for specific tasks.	**£6,350 to £8,400**	£6,985 to £9,240
(c)	Itching, irritation of and/or rashes on one or both hands, but resolving within a few months with treatment.	**£1,250 to £2,900**	£1,375 to £3,190

13

Minor Injuries

Minor injuries are injuries which are of short duration, where there is a complete recovery within three months and are not otherwise referred to in other chapters. Cases where there is significant pain or multiple injuries albeit full recovery within three months may fall outside this chapter. Likewise cases involving, for example, travel anxiety (associated with minor physical injuries) or minor scarring where symptoms last for more than three months may appropriately be included in this chapter. The awards within each bracket will be dependent on the severity and duration of symptoms. The extent to which the level of symptoms remains relatively constant will also be a relevant factor.

			with 10% uplift
(a)	Injuries where there is a complete recovery within seven days.	**A few hundred pounds to £500**	A few hundred pounds to £550
(b)	Injuries where there is a complete recovery within 28 days.	**£500 to £1,000**	£550 to £1,100
(c)	Injuries where there is a complete recovery within three months.	**£1,000 to £1,800**	£1,100 to £1,980

Index